THIS

this

Andy Weaver

CHAUDIERE BOOKS MMXV

Can one not suppose, therefore, that the book is not solely, indeed not at all, a vehicle of or support for communication? It isn't a medium: it is immediately, itself, above all else, communication and commerce of itself with itself.

Jean-Luc Nancy, *On the Commerce of Thinking: Of Books and Bookstores*

"WHEN THE POINT IS TO TRY TO PRESENT THAT THERE IS SOMETHING THAT IS NOT PRESENTABLE, YOU HAVE TO MAKE PRESENTATION SUFFER."

JEAN-FRANÇOIS LYOTARD, "REPRESENTATION, PRESENTATION, UNPRESENTABLE"

"TO EXIST IS ONE THING, TO BE PERCEIVED ANOTHER."

SUSAN HOWE, "ARISBE"

"THIS BOOK IS INTERESTING AS THERE IS AS MUCH FAILURE AS SUCCESS IN IT."

GERTRUDE STEIN, "A TRANSATLANTIC INTERVIEW"

THIS IS THE MOST IMPORTANT THINGS:

This this this this. This is where you think it is.
–Ron Silliman, *Ketjak, The Age of Huts (Compleat)* [p 46]

this is a sign to
someone here

the sky and drinking
by light & your brain
by its processes

are ears which are
deaf to a self
they hear they are

blind too
in the unbridgeable gulf
called

the this
–Steve McCaffery, *Evoba,* p 74

This: a flaw it is that I talk like: This
–Dorothy Trujillo Lusk, "The Worst"

This suspension. This this.
–Clark Coolidge, "Our"

THIS IS THE PARTICULAR:

Those legs & knees,
that throat exactly,
that chin, those hands & feet, that hair she loved
are not rejected, not blotted out,
but
are the steps by which her love moves from
the single, the individual to everything
alive
–Hilda Morley, "The Steps"

You may not want to
but you know – as well as I –
this is the limit
–Cid Corman, *nothing doing*

This is Robert Creeley
–Robert Creeley, "Heroes"

I can't say it any more clearly than this
–Lisa Robertson, "A Cuff"

This is just to say
–William Carlos Williams

This is the & of the world
–Caroline Bergvall, "Cogs"

THIS IS NOT A WORD.
THIS IS TO SAY.
THIS IS A PATTERN OF INK.

THIS IS HOW THE WORD WORLDS

Words
are
pleasure.
All
words.
Robert Creeley, Pieces

now then
is so
when but howevers
its ifs
what whats
throughout
and none the less
lessens the this

why not if why so
maybe or no
but still a there
so much in here
with its and
and its with

so yes
yes
just this
just so

CONTENT / THISIS STATEMENT / THISTORY LESSON

This is / Thisis / Thiiss

politics,

concatenations,

s s a l G l a s s
      l   l
    a   l   a
  s   s
s   a   s

        s

        s

This
goes

without
saying

"Language becomes a gift we give each other in the communis, for no other purpose save that we can." Dani Spinosa, *[Generic Pronoun] Creates*

dear reader,
a nerd drew an awed werd,
drew a ward nervy and ravened,
revved dawn and yawned a
weary dawn away.

A year yawned and waned,
day wavered anew.
an aery raven weaved and warned
an ever wary deer.
Raw ear and eye
added a wry and rare
yarn. A darned
nerve ended
war, a vender wavered
and averred a dewy, wan
era. Rend a dead warren,
weave a dray, and wend
a raw, weedy navy

Rave and deny
read and dye
reed and
wed a dew
waver anew.

new yen rarely earned,
wave an award near any renderer

```
yawler

   zinging
  along
   bob

  creeley
     doing
everything

fast
     going

here
       immanence
    jokingly
       knarled
   lacking
    maxims
   nothing
    over
   passing
quotidian
rudder
   sending

  to
unto
 verifying
   with

x
```

ssalGlass

You know, in language we inherit the voices of the dead. Language is passed on to us by people who are now in their graves and brings with it access to history, tradition, times and places that are not at all immediate to our own immediate and particular occasion whether we look at it individually and personally or whether we look at it in a more collective way and talk about a specific community.

Nathaniel Mackey ("Interview by Edward Foster" 276)

Things one sees through
a blurred sheet of glass,
that figures, predestined,
conditions of thought.

Robert Creeley, "Rain"

The warm wind through the multitude, the many, the dry oceans moving in their slow crests. Breathless shock of morning, trapping air between the pains. Grain falls from top to bottom, bottom to top, each second touched by pursed lips. A focus of intent leaves the world burning, a bow offers wine, a resounding noise of ringynge or trumpynge. Who is the hero of the autoclave's silence? The questions of bees, the confusion of birds, the latinate despair of Prague. The calmness of the lake and its tadpoled secrets of wonder. Opera. Phillip. Wine. Stained. And all the time Alice looking. Frozen organics of stem and flute. The acute area of sight, the most aesthetic of aerodynamics. The shepherd's delight, dial, weather, and time, the true name of still. Temperature's annealing strength, change as an agent of permanence. The whorls, loops, and arches of science. The parison dreams imagination fires. The proper door to every hue of light. Blood is a superb conductor but not of electricity. The verbness of shine. How to best bend the breath, how to cup blood to the surface, how to vitrify. The heart is no easy symbol but a pale grey organ, drunk on dreams of blood. For fish, the boundary of the universe is a peak into dry matter. Women banging the tops of their heads in shock. Chagall is the only man to follow, his hands naming the colours of light. Always half full or half empty, either or. Simplest lesson of binary logic. The unbearable insomnia of wind. The bond and the breaking stick. Whole histories of fleeting desire pass through you, silent, Thamyris the Thracian, a singer without memory. Volcanic birth of obsidian. Language's opaque touch. The shards of the body, their anarchic desire for freedom. Ambivalence, in the wall but not of it, never inside or out. Putting the ass back in sight. Our delicate menageries. Suggestions to "Take your hare when it is cased" fall deafly on Hannah's ears. A packaged touchstone, sand and soda for surrounding time. Knowledge of egg's speed in hot water. Correction of eyes. Distance of stars, shapes of the moon's scars, the red pride of a cardinal from hundreds of feet. The thrusting passion of mercury. The calmness of a silent sea. The shineness of verb. Touché. The translator's embarrassment as he slips away in his slippers of fur, and the secret joy of the princess of waiting. How to show a woman's foot gracefully, perhaps gradually. The very definition of a resounding noise. Bees in a voyeur's hive. Preserving summer for the tongue. How the scotch fluted into the warmth of our hands. The tempered fear of the glazier's breath. How the cricket views his shrilling organ. So much of the old folks' blues whispered through your grinning mouth. Where the coal-fish hides his name. Where language stops is not where the unsayable occurs, but rather where the matter of words begins. The lunette flourish of time, parison holding the petals of the passing seconds. A pipette's delicate pull, and the surface tension of skin over the open mouth. Sensual neck of retort; the absurd weightiness of metal and earthenware, the absolute temerity of perspex. Pure, molten fluidity before the photochromic taint. Good natured schooner of joy on the coaster. Mortification, punishment, *Sturm und Drang* of ascension, silica's vitrification to the right hand of the Lord. Glittering transubstantiation. This Platonic ideal of breath. The brittleness of innocence, the idea of matter. Do you share the weep holes' despair? *Love, I must die, I faint, close up my*

this

this
   sings

this
   singing

this
   sings
    ing

unrestrained
vocalization
wantonly
xerocopies
yeasty
zaibatsu
always
buy
conversation
diddles
exchange
fiddles
garish
humanism
innocuously
jovially
kneels
liquidity
manufactures
nonfunctional
oralities
produces
quietizing
rabbits
subterfuging
tophats

zoogyroscope's
agile
bushy-tailed
canid
deftly
escapes
foxes
greyhounds
hurdles
in flagrante delicto
jerrymandering
koine
lexicon
modified
new
options
possible
quotient
rendered
sensible
talk's
unknowable
vulpes
wordcraft's
xenagogic

YHWH

The northbound lanes of Interstate 29 were closed for several hours early Monday after a truck hauling 30,000 lbs. of windows lost control and overturned in the right hand lane. The truck, owned by Anderson Trucking of Fargo, was headed to Marvin Windows in Warroad, Minn. The driver, Matthew Skalet, 37, of Moorhead, was transported to Altru hospital where he was treated for minor injuries. Limiting sparkling wines to celebratory aperitif or dessert duty shortchanges them. They can complement any food: oysters, lobster, roast duck, grilled vegetables, risotto or a plate of buttery cheeses. As the tasting panel worked through an assortment of American sparkling wines, Eric Asimov remarked that they would be delicious with fried chicken. That was my very thought. Sparkling wine makes a wonderful match with fried food, because the acidity in the wine and its lively carbonation balance the fat, cleansing the palate for the next luscious bite. These wines give fried chicken a bright, clean partner.   IN SPACE, SURFACE TENSION RUINS OUR ONE-GRAVITY GAGS.   *A pale green Israeli unguentarium from 200* AD. *There are no cracks or chips, the vessel is in excellent condition. Found in the Holy Land. There is a partial covering of dirt inside and out. Built as a vial for tears.*   UNITY APPEARS TO BE A ONE-WAY STREET IN ILLINOIS AND DESTROYING GOOD PEOPLE IS THE ONLY REMAINING SKILL OF OUR DYING.   THE MAELSTROM OF WAR EXISTS AS A TOURIST ATTRACTION.   *The horses charged at us. Over 100 protesters were injured. Tensions rose, and we broke through the police ranks on to the lawn of the embassy, tearing up the plastic fence and uprooting hedges. We threw stones, smoke bombs and fireworks. Ugly scenes followed.*   A BEATING COBRA'S HEART TO BE DRUNKEN WITH WINE.   *Vietnam is the most heavily bombed country in history, but it is a country, not a war.*   *Disoriented children screamed to get out, not enjoying the feeling of being buried alive.*   *Cows and buffaloes, accompanied by the screeching of corroded brakes, reluctantly amble off the road at the last possible moment.*   *A guidebook had advised to 'just have complete faith the steady torrent of motorcycle traffic will dodge you as you cross from one side to the other'.*   *I took a taxi. Drivers are shrunken, leathery men wearing frayed baseball caps turned sideways. And the sign said: 'Please do not pay in case meter is out of work; just pay exactly for the total amount on meter.' I paid what he asked.* *I asked him about the war and got the expected answer: 'Which war?' I asked him about government repression, and he explained how state censorship, enforced amnesia and the consequent death of journalism invariably increase the significance of fiction and poetry. Vietnam has a high literacy rate. Streets with small libraries are named after poets, and daily newspapers publish short stories and poems. But, he added: 'There is still a shortage of paper, ink, and the freedom to publish.' Tuan walked me to one of his ancestor's graves, which stood proudly in the centre of the rice field. I asked him to translate the epitaph. He could not: it was in an ideographic language that France had destroyed.* *Tuan carefully navigated though the waterborne bustle of floating markets and bobbing boats until we landed at a tourist complex where we could buy ethnic trinkets, US Army petrol lighters, lacquerware and ceramics and sample fresh fruits, snake wine and honey. I bought a lampshade hat and started gorging myself.* *If a dish made with any of the above ingredients seems tame, wash it down with a cup of rice wine into which a freshly cut out, still beating cobra's heart is gently and lovingly dropped.* *Saigon – city of colonial and erotic, exotic, chaotic, narcotic adventure, Vietnam's Big Bad Apple, the world's fast-food capital, epicentre of male fantasy – throbs day and night. Elegant ladies sitting ramrod straight on dainty mopeds, wearing long white gloves and flapping robes, swiftly glided by. Women in invisible miniskirts rode side-saddle out of motorbike wash shops, their lustrous long hair streaming behind them.* *In a street devoted to selling guitars, next to a small Buddhist temple where people prayed for the success of a new karaoke bar, a photocopying stand, or a good crop, I stopped at a makeshift cafe hastily erected in a covered entrance to a warehouse. Just outside, two pigs frolicked in a puddle, and a woman lay on an irregular, jagged pavement being lovingly massaged.* AN ABHORRENCE FOR BOXED WINE. RAISED OVER THE HEAD OF THE VICTIM, ABOUT TO BE EMBEDDED IN HIS HEAD AND HIS EAR, A SCAR ON HIS ARM FOR LIFE. *Traffic on Interstate 29 was detoured Monday between DeMers Avenue and Gateway Drive as crews worked to clear more than 20,000 pounds of broken windows and a wrecked semi from the roadway. The semi, northbound on I-29 to deliver a load of panes to Marvin Windows and Doors in Warroad, Minn., slid across the interstate about 5 A.M., after its driver reached for something and lost control of the vehicle, authorities said. The driver suffered injuries and was transported to Altru Hospital, where he was treated and released Monday morning. He was cited for "care required in operation of a motor vehicle."*

The body bleeds only water and fear when you survive
the death of your politics,
Dionne Brand, *Land to Light On*

Politics

I,
too,
dislike it: there are things that are important beyond this fiddle.
The gnattering on of flies, an old man holding his wig
against the wind. Has the shipwreck of the singular
stayed news? Siding on the err of caution. What does not change
is time, the only element of change. I understand
times are tough, but, really now, dark *days*
of the soul? I can't see the polis for the me's.
Too often defined for others by others. As surely
as Saturday night must trade with Sunday morning,
the law of squirrel and acorn, willow branch and wet
wind, west wind with north and south with east.

georgian
hacks
invariably

just

knew
literature
manifested
noblesse
oblige
poetry
quadrated
rightfully
squared
titleship
undeniable
verse
wilfully
xeriscaped
yowling
zigzagging
accounts
binding
consensus
differends
entrenched
furtively

heare
theire
theise

wordage's
xanthopsial
yogibogeyboxes
zither
around
because
catoptric
deflections
evoke
falsiloquence
grammaring
hosts
ingest
jejune
kindle-talk
loquaciously
mirroring
nominally
out-of-date
primers'
quantophrenia
re
stupefying
tabescent
unspeakable
verbiage

Politics

The Dow is up, taxes are down, people are happy.
Those are hard answers to question.
And what would happen if we put our mouths
where our money is? As if I haven't puckered up,
closed my eyes, and bobbed my head on a strange man's
bill roll. *We manufacture consolations here in America*
while there are probably not a dozen men fighting
in Europe who did not long ago give up
every reason for their being there except that nobody
knew how to get them away. Whatever I might say,
I'm most truly marked by the politics of the expanding
waistline. Most of the time, the most political I get
is the more homey miracles: the changing of wine into
urine, the eating of loaves and fishes to feed
this mass. Since war is the health of the state,
it's easier to think of some governments as fitness nuts.
Not much—
just sitting around, putting the loser in illusory.
I used to dream of being a barking dog.
Randolph Bourne died of Spanish Flu.

Politics

The Kantian sublime dwells in the muscles
of the human forearm, the open hand
curling in its five fingers.

I title this diary *Sorrows of a Little Quietest.*
Pass me that banjo, I want to play another verse of
Pity the Poor Middle Class White Man Blues. Yeah, he's got
them *The Prime Rate's Going to Raise My Suburban
Mortgage Blues* real bad. Can you dig his *I'm So Far Down
I Might Have to Sell the Second Boat* blues?
Everyone loves to hear him play the *My Pension Plan
Is Down Slightly Blues.* Rumour has it, he sold his soul
at the crossroads for a menoporsche and a better tax shelter.

Yeah! Put your hands together for Weaver's
First-World-Problem Blues Band, singing their latest hit,
"Self-Directed Irony (is Our Holy Shield)."

i

am

one

am

i

fictions
generate
hope
intoxicated
judgment
kowtows
logorrhea
minding
not
our

p's
q's

receiving
several
things
unexamined
vox
wholly
x'd
yields
zymotic
abdication
bread
circuses
deepdished
empiry

jowly
Kremlinologists
like
mynahs
nonstop
otiosely
proposed
questions
reimagined
squat
their
unctuous
vengeful
word-stock
Xeroxed
yester-year's
Zhdanovism
abrading
basal
cerebration
dry-rotting
efficacious
foundations
glad-handing
howlers
interminably

In the hands of Robert Hooke, the first step to germ theory. *Micrographia* as the founding of infectious disease research. A world invisible to the naked eye. A lack of origin discovered by accident-prone Phoenicians. Cooking pots placed on a sandy beach in the middle of Egypt or Mesopotamia. Syrian craftsmen blowing the Romans a brittle kiss. The early death-knell of wineskins, a substitute for precious stones. Mongol incursions into Russia and Islamic territories setting back the cause for centuries. Mathematics and optics coming into plain sight in the 13th century. *A reflection of variations in climate, drinking habits, availability of pottery, and political events. Accidents instigated the movement of western societies around the knowledge-innovation-quantification triangle.* Microscopes, telescopes, barometers, thermometers, vacuum flasks, retort flasks, and many others. Literally turning western civilization from an aural to a visual mode of interpreting experience, thus a cell death for certain of the mind's faculties. Thomson's discovery of electrons, Faraday's work on electricity, Newton's splitting of white light into colors with a prism. Some argue this is the reason that the knowledge revolution of the last 500 years took place in western Europe and not in Islamic civilizations, in India, Japan, and China. Others argue not. Others argue knowledge revolts at the perfect rate needed by its society. I do not read Japanese, Chinese, Hindi or Punjabi; most of my others did not care to. Histology, pathology, protozoology, bacteriology, and molecular biology. Astronomy, physics, mineralogy, engineering, paleontology, vulcanology, and geology all molded into their perfect shape. No steam engine, no internal combustion engine, no electricity, no light bulbs, no cameras, and no television? Merely silence or two people talking face to face? Barbarism, Luddite, to cheer for the Visigoths. Debate: one imperfect shape matched to another, voice as a square peg in the human ear's round hole. The birth of a new understanding of infectious disease. Spectacles overtaking the nosegay. Chemistry elucidated the lost Europe of nitrogen, gone in the haze of its ammonia fertilizers, a huge step forward. By no means demonstrating the structure of the solar system, stellar parallax substantiated that Copernicus altered our concept of cosmology. No one over 50 will be able to read this unforeseen accident, the movement of your fingers around the triangle delta. Galileo angered the Church by exposing the manufacture of innovative artifacts followed their mass production. Urban planning offers eight ways of declining knowledge. The discovery of DNA offers no way to substantiate the conjectures of Copernicus and Galileo. So much depends heavily upon instrumentation. Thanks to European scientists who elucidated the chemistry of nitrogen and learned to fix this gas in the form of ammonia to produce artificial nitrogenous fertilizers, a huge step forward in 19th- and 20th-century agriculture. Without, no means to demonstrate the structure of the solar system, no measurement of stellar parallax, no way to substantiate Galileo. The revolutionized understanding of cell division completely altering our concept of cosmology. No understanding of deep space, no genetics, and no discovery of DNA. No one knows if we would have had Polish Jews tuning instruments next to barbed wire audiences. Cells. Division.

english
french
german
hebrew

italian
japanese
kashmiri
latin
mandarin
norwegian
ojibwe
persian
quechua
russian
spanish
tuvan
urdu
valencian
welsh
xhosa
yiddish

zulu
all
belie
constructed
denaturings

this is

not knotnought
nought knotnot
knot notnought

Politics

Duncan said the job was to imagine
not oppose evil, to plumb and understand and not throw up
another evil to fight burning with fire.
Olson, channelling Confucius, reminds us that
nothing is possible without doing it. Goodness, like evil,
is an action. This is the one order humanity must admit:
I was just as likely to release the gas
as scrape my nails against the doors.
This machine, a recent convert to the liberal cause,
now prefers to engage fascists in a healthy dialogue
about the opportunities for wealth inherent in free-market
capitalism. Autumn has exposed the arthritic reachings
of the old oak trees. America, go improve yourself
with a healthy 401K.

Try to imagine evil? In this world, how can we not?

möbius
nooses
ouroboros
passageways
quote
ratiocination's
stealing
thoughts
unquote
verbal
wisdom's
xograph
yelloched
zestily
across
brain
candy
doughnutting
eight
figures
governing
hullabaloo's
infinite
jest
kickbacked
looking-glass
möbius

k k
n n nn
o o
tu tt u
g g
h h
t t

k
nnn
ooo
ttut
g
h
t

k k
n n
o o
u t tu
g g
h h
t t

We have discussed science from 1200 on; all knowledge was interconnected. The Renaissance based on a pile of sand and ash. Venetians showing us to ourselves, showing the best of ourselves to God. To discuss da Vinci is to see coloured light in the hands of the Blessed Virgin. Startling changes that Durer wrote as the laws of our sight. Utilitarian element to some. Certainly the cause of much birth and much death. A flower growing in the era's mind. Molten liquid transforming agriculture, horticulture, and the length of the working day. A revolution in consumer capitalism, surely for the best of the largest number of shopkeepers. Perspective of our unknown desires offered to us in every aspect of everyday life. House dirt becoming more apparent in improved light. The precocious growth of fruit, and vegetables covering the house. The 19th century made it possible to bring plants from all over the world to enrich European farms and gardens. Cloches covering the land with Roman ideas of health and hygiene. Clean them out before they dirty us.

quicquidlibet
realisticicizing
serpents
toodle
up-buttering
very
wide-eyed
xenoparasitic
yeomen
zabernism
aver
bosses
cryptarchic
diction
effectively
facilizes
governmental
helotage
indignatios
jargogle
knowables
literally
malaprops
narcotize
obfuscations
pacificate

To think and perceive, a tool that improves every day. When the Visigoths charged, the Romans protected their grapes. *This, however, is not saddening; or rather, it is only for an enquiry which, mistaking one question for another, continues to ask What?, where not only are there no more answers, but no longer any questions either.* The period saw many changes, a healthier diet to the people. To each their own. I required the heart-shaped bauble and a strong mallet. The sextant required the precision chronometer invented by Harrison in 1714. *The truly saddening thing would be if final knowledge still had the form of an object.* Up till 1713, the sea required nothing but aimless navigation and travel to offer its tireless punchline. Jeffers's eye stared back into space and offered tears to no one. A revolution in drinking habits as bottles transported beer and wine. Stained additions to the fascination and mystery of light and the drunkard's desire to study optics. The shift from a line to a series of dots. *The drift toward this definitive closure of truth...* says Agamben. Windows, through lanterns, lighthouses, and greenhouses, through cameras and television, our world emerged from a sea of shards held momentarily together in rich interconnections, and the waiting mallet. *Precisely the absence of any final object of knowledge saves us from the irremediable sadness of things.* Hands cup under the faucet, the watch face watches, the fingers let go and water covers the floor.

This is a small poem for Robert Kroetsch, as a belated thanks for those pints of beer that day he visited Fredericton in the Fall of 1995

This poem, in accordance with the laws of Newtonian physics, laws that guide the apotheosis of coal, that lie behind the spin of heavenly bodies at the far reaches of redshifting space in exactly the same degree as the dancing interplay of butterflies and western winds pillaging cherry blossoms to the sea coast or the concatenation of lovers, that thrust rocks incessantly up to beat against the farmer's harrow, against the sea coast covered in cherry blossoms and wind-battered butterflies, that are the unknowable whirls that scientists as much as priests understand as the whorls on the fingertips of a god lost in its machinations and neglecting its duties of miracles for thousands of years or else intimate in these laws and in all of life from the grain of sand to the stained glass windows of Chartres and so everything rests constantly in the divine inspiration of life, composing itself in the smallest and grandest theogonies, brakes for chicks.

Politics

There are many ways to measure
the distance between the full hand
and the empty belly. Why, yes, I would
buy wine on the recommendation of an
attractive young woman in a top hat
and fishnet stockings. There's a reason
why it's not called flow-down economics.
I know you love me, Capitalism, but can't we
stay just friends? Yea, again I tell you, it is easier
for a fat man to waddle through the bend
of the golden arches than for a poor man
to enter the kingdom of heaven
and satiate his desire for breaded
reconstituted chicken parts.

harmony

is
jazzy
key
lay
music's
nonce
orchestrates
procreates
questing
rhythms
speaks
tempos
unheard
vivifying
wordings'
xenium
yet
zealously
atonal
boys
conjointly
deserve
every
fudging
goodness

olson's
proprioceptive
quintessence
realized
spontaneously
tissue's
unaccountable
verities
wanderlusting
xerographies
yearning
zeitgeber
almost
becoming
cutaneous
decalescence
ensemble's
filial
genetic
handprint
in
jamboree
kinoplasm
launching
moment's
notice

```
Aaaa  aaaa-aaaa  aaaaaaaaaa'a  aaaaaaa
Bbbb  bbbb-bbbb  bbbbbbbbbb'b  bbbbbbb
Cccc  cccc-cccc  cccccccccc'c  ccccccc
Dddd  dddd-dddd  dddddddddd'd  ddddddd
Eeee  eeee-eeee  eeeeeeeeee'e  eeeeeee
Ffff  ffff-f ff   f fffffff'f  fffffff
Gggg  gggg-g gg   g ggggggg'g  ggggggg
Hhhh  hhhh-h hh   h hhhhhh 'h  hhhhhh
I ii  i ii-i ii   i iii ii 'i  iii ii
J  j  j  j-j jj   j jjj  j 'j  jjj  j
K  k  k  k-k kk   k kkk  k 'k  kkk  k
L  l  l  l-l ll   l lll  l 'l  lll  l
M  m  m  m-m mm   m mmm  m 'm  mmm  m
N  n  n  n-n nn   n nnn  n 'n  nnn  n
O  o  o  o-  oo   o ooo    'o   oo
P  p  p  p-  pp   p ppp    'p    p
Q  q  q  q-  qq   q qqq    'q    q
R  r  r  r-  rr   r rrr    'r    r
S  s  s  s-  ss   s  ss    's    s
T     t     -       t  tt    '     t
          -       u  u     '
          -       v  v     '
          -          w     '
          -          x     '
          -          y     '
          -                '
```

Shape molten honey-like into flowers, flamework a vibrant bead. A suncatcher. Personal fuse an original design. Tell me more, this hands-on activity. Techniques create their own objects: a flower at the furnace, beads at the torch, pieces made in the hotshop and flameshop of the fevered few. Everything else from the coldworking shop, freezing in our cultural climate. Decorate an object by cutting, grinding, and polishing, a rotating wheel and abrasives. Metallic stain for the human form. Geometric ornament, vegetal motifs, calligraphy—the three building blocks of Islamic art. Copper produces red or brown, silver produces yellow, a hallmark of early Islamic presence in Egypt. Sasanian craftsmen shining like Muhammad in 622, a craftsman resembling rock crystal of eggshell thinness. A cut and colour gone out of fashion. Festooned, featherlike patterns were restrained, gilded flamboyant century illuminating the interiors of mosques. Artistic imagination and technical expertise gilding the very dust with liquid medium. In the later Middle Ages, Europeans prized Islamic luxuries because of their exotic appearance and technical sophistication, and sometimes because they were believed to be relics from the Holy Land. Fragments of Islam unearthed in archeological excavations all over Europe, and some are contained in cathedral treasuries. One mission accomplished. Inflated molten of purple, blue, and green, white trails festooning into featherlike tails. Object relief. Cut and colour out of fashion, restrained flamboyance of gilt and enamel. Brilliant polychrome ornaments hanging lamps that illuminate the interiors of mosques. Artistic imagination and technical expertise, the dog wagging the tail and the tail wagging the air. Sand shifts under the feet of Egyptian craftsmen, while the Nile flows like the tongue of God. Gold dust and liquid medium. Avoid

THE DANGERS OF COLORS, EACH WITH ITS SLIGHTLY DIFFERENT TEMPERATURE. EVERYTHING FIXED IN THE FURNACE. IN THE MIDDLE AGES, EUROPEANS PRIZED ISLAMIC LUXURY. A BEAKER WITH MANY DIFFERENT BIRDS. IMPORTANT PATRONS WHOSE DATES ARE UNKNOWN. THE INSCRIPTION OF LAMPS ON RELICS FROM THE HOLY LAND, THE BOWL AND THE FLASK IN CATHEDRAL TREASURIES. IRAN'S SWAN'S NECK ROSEWATER SPRINKLER AN IMPORTANT CLUE ON THE PASSAGE TO CHINA. A DISTINCT EUROPEAN INFLUENCE, ENGLAND EXPORTED TO INDIA. EXAMPLES FROM THE OTTOMAN EMPIRE KNOWN ONLY FROM ILLUSTRATIONS IN MANUSCRIPTS. AT LEAST ONE TURKISH MASTER TRAINED FOR CUTTING AND GILDING IN VENICE. EVEN EXPERTS HAVE DIFFICULTY DISTINGUISHING HIS PRODUCTS. MOORISH DECORATION FOR MARKETS CLOSER TO HOME. PRESERVATION OF A WAY OF ELEGANT EXAMPLE.

[this]
english
[this]
virus
[this]
arti
fice

A uniform of arguable phase where the word is produced when the viscous material cools too rapidly below its transition temperature. Molten time forms a crystal lattice under tension, a biologically inactive material breaks into shards. Sharp force withstands the heat treatment. Compound the household into smooth and impervious objects. Vicious by weight, the light bulbs into magnolia trees in spring. The fountain babbles at the cardinals, the cardinals both peck at the scattered seeds and have the pope's ear. Without sufficient time, even spring is lost, swine gnaw at the pearls. A great amount of force. Raw material sticks in the craw. The properties of farce can be modified or changed where the word is used to describe the familiar form. To some, lead is no less a form of lead, just as to others water is no less a form of wine. Whether ashes or dust is the major raw material, the old cat waddles under the bed and refuses to be dragged to the sunlight. Depleted before production, depleted after production, depleted during production, solidarity forever remains a pretty song.   Pure major material almost quartz in form. Although it is almost pure, it contains amounts of colour depleted before production reduces the molten from the common method for the most expensive classes. Fingers form a fist, the workers form a union. On top of the tin, the name floats its own noumenal template. Few own greenhouses. Many more own hammers.

concatenations
dictate
easy
figurations
gaudy
highlights
invest
jerkwater
kaleidoscopic
lexemes
mit
noesis
obliquely
prehending
quodammodotative
reality
sublimely
traced
unbreachable
varsal
worlds
x-irradiated
yestern
zeitgeists
alwise
bedevilling

this
tells
me
the
shadow
of
the
crow
cannot
be
the
crow's
shadow

Politics

The oak tree doesn't care
whose lot its leaves fall on.
Say what you will about Freddy Krueger,
it's nice to see a man take pride in his work.
Don't you think it's suspicious no one's ever
seen Karl Marx and Bill Gates in the same place
at the same time? I mean, I'm not saying.
I'm just saying. Even when the mind
isn't minding, the brain is still braining.
After the long days of rain,
the first robins begin to sing.
By all means, write beautiful testimonials to love.
Standards of economy dictate that a girl
dead at five has lived a whole life.
He's got money to burn
you. Let's bomb them back to the Flintstone age.
Who knows why democracy doesn't work?
The earthworm lobby wants to know
when last week's rainstorm and every
grade twelve biology class will be declared
a state of emergency. Perhaps Marx's great
insight was that a scared world is really not
different from a sacred one. I take great comfort
in knowing that when I die the multinational
corporations will go on without me.

ideation
jargonizes
knowledge
langue
masks
nothingology
obtenebrating
parole
quiescently
Realpolitik
shifts
the
unspoken
vernacular
weakens
xenocracy
yawps
zombification
accomplished
bemuted
citizens
drag
employed
feet
globalizing
heedlessly

A piece of obsidian, naturally occuring since the stone age. Pliny the Elder tells his fanboy stories of the Phoenicians. A merchant ship moored without stones to prop their pots, the sands of the shore steamed and flowed. A fortuitous meal. Thus was the origin. A translucent liquid from an opaque mind. Archaeological evidence supports many claims, a picture frame covers many marriages. A timepiece ticks the hours from the ship to Mesopotamia and beaded decorations discover the same Native American architectures. From green to bluish green, from sea to shining sea, the sand blushes to produce its blinding impurities. Gem-cutters from Egypt collected light of brilliant hues. Blue beads were believed to have magical powers in the ancient New Kingdom, 1500 BC. A variety of puzzles remain as our trading commodities with the past. A melding of naturally occurring iron wound around molten metal bars. Ekphrasis is a crutch for feeble bards, tongues in their mouths like pieces of obsidian left over from the stone age. The marriage cup seals one of many deals. Greece is open for trade, traitorous winds will blow sand just as well. Gemstones of brilliant red, green, and blue under a flag awaiting its colours. Is nothing more highly prized than a saleable democracy? Egyptian thread centres the minotaur. Fishing for string with a bag of sand knotted to the end of a rod. Colourful decorations removed from a wound in the statue's side, a Roman cup pouring molten beads into a mould. Technology spread to Greece and beyond. Decorations coloured the eastern end of the Mediterranean for seven centuries, covered only by the free-blowing sand. Such tedious guilt often hampers the survivors. Through conquest and trade, enamelling, staining, and gilding spread as far as Scandinavia and the British Isles. Ornate processes of domination twinkle in the evening sunlight. Common through the centuries until usage declined and certain techniques were forgotten, but production did not completely stop. Thick windows manufacture an obedient will. After the fall of the empire, Constantine moved to Byzantium and continued on. Artists gathered in the folds of the valley like pebbles on the beach and the most beautiful vases resulted. Potash opening the world. Torcello, that scented link to Venice. White pebbles and burnt vegetation in the south, smouldering wood ashes in the north. A burnt offering to stain light with metallic impurities surely divides God's Church in two. Islamic Spain was the first to turn its eyes back to its own eyes. Venice learned to smooth the waves, but, translucent or flat, shapes will show through the sphere. The trick is to cut while still hot. God blowing the spheres into perfect concentricity. The aeolian harp, the wind chimes, the block of ice thawing on Cage's piano strings. The flaw left in the rug. The Crown's moulding, casting, and breaking, a globe pounded flat for the sake of simplicity. Impurities for colour, metal for flavour. A rolled plate as the symbol of the century. A lucrative export trade in luxury items, the island of Murano the short-lived centre of a world shining in the sun. Local quartz pebbles ground into the currency of light. The makers were soon the most prominent citizens and weren't allowed to leave the Republic. An entire industry built on the fear of fire, the city's mostly wooden buildings driving a monopoly of risk. Murano's reputation poled through the streets of Venice as masters slipped into the English night. Local differences almost pure as a fine sand mirrored the surrounding waters. Grains fall apart; the centre can but hold; mere precession is loosed upon the world. Choose your own adventure: turn to soteriology or theodicy?

this summer

cicadas
      sang
 rain sprang
   ones twained
            and twained

Lo
morphemes'
nostrum
overzealous
panacea
quicksilvers
referents'
sea-like
translations
until
vitreous
words'
xerophytic
Yggdrasils
zoomorphize
alien
brain-boxes
circumferencing
dictionarially
entire
fields'
groundwork
hardwiring
imagination's
jouissance
kitschily

back
channels
disappear
Eleusinian
foretunes
garbled
hidden
Iacchus
Jesuitocratized
Kore
liturgized
mysterious
novices
offered
purifications
quarantined
rabidly
stricken
tiring
under
vocabulary's
waxing
xenodiagnosis
yeaning
zygote
Alpha-virus

this
is
not
the
three
thrushes
there
their
three
hushes

speech
tracking
umbilical
vestigials

wordbound
xiphopagi
yammering
zero-morphic
abstractions
block
change
deictic
evasions
flair
gyrating
hind-like
inside
jabberwock
kafkaesquely
logos
manipulates
noumenal
operations
patrolled
quickly
refrained

Politics

Old Bill, at your age, to turn to the world
(to *keep* turning to the world) only
to see, with Char, to believe, at your age,
that beauty will right all things. This faith
in your imagination, your power to naturalize,
to acclimate, to choose the yellow flower
for your very own—it's both
inspiring and unseemly. No defeat is made up
entirely of defeat, you say. There is no other
fit medium of address, you say. A new world
is only a new mind, you say. At your age!
Even at my age, I'm uncertain—is it a good thing
that I can do nothing but sing about it and so
be assuaged from my pain? Wouldn't the wheel
barrows say something entirely else? Still,
at least you were still looking for the right answers.
On my best days, I ask the wrong questions.

This
is
what
upon
so
much
wheel
barrow
de
pends

dead
etymology's
flickering
ghosts
haunt
impairing
justifications
knot
liminality
mawkish
nouns
open
punctilious
quietus
remanded
sublime
time
undergoes
vulgar
woading
Xronos
yoked
zero-summed
a
body
cenotaphic

A SMALL SCRATCH ON THE MIND RELEASING THE ATOMIC BONDS. THE THEORY IS THAT IT SHOULD BE FIVE TIMES STRONGER THAN STEEL BUT INTERNAL STRESSES LOSE THE STRENGTH. FROZEN INSIDE, BURSTING THROUGH THE COLD SKIN, THE TADPOLE'S BULBOUS END CAN ENDURE THE HAMMER'S BLOW. ONLY CHILDREN AND SCIENTISTS DARE TEST THE KING'S GRANDSON'S THEORY. A 17TH-CENTURY DRAWING OF THE AMAZED COURTIER HOLDING A HANDFUL OF POWDER CAN BE SEEN ABOVE. EXPECTING JAGGED SHARDS PROTECTS THE SURFACE FROM THE SHATTERING SCRATCH OF REALITY, THE ATOMIC RELEASE OF THE MIND. A SMALL SOB PUSHED INTO COLD WATER, COOLED BY THE WATER IN A THIN, FRAGILE TALE FOR THE TELLER TO DELICATELY HOLD. WHAT IS A HARMLESS JOKE TO A KING IS A MATTER OF CONCERN FOR THE COURT. A JOKE IN THE RIGHT HAND, THE HAND THAT WIELDS POWDER. RELAX, BUT DO NOT SLUMP; ANNEAL THE SKIN SLOWLY TO SEE THE PRETTIEST COLOURS. EVEN THE DIARIST UNDERSTANDS THE WORKINGS OF POWER. *Some of them froft, but the body falls not into pieces; others break into pieces, a fmall noife, before the red heat be over; others foon after the red heat is over, and with a great noife; fome neither break nor crack, till they feem to be quite cold; others keep whole whileft they are in the water, and fly to pieces of themfelves with a fmart noife....* THE THREAD, THE BODY, THE NECK, AND THE POINT OF THE NEEDLE. LYE AND THE METAL ROD. POWDER, NOT JAGGED PIECES. WE TEND TO HAVE LESS STRENGTH THAN THEORY WOULD SUGGEST.

Politics

Let's take this show on the road. How poor is he?
He's so poor he's not even properly alienated
from his own labour! Knock-knock! Who's
there? When is a soccer stadium like a torture
chamber? When is a soccer stadium like a torture
chamber who? Chile, 1973. That act won't play
in the States. I mean, I care as much as the next person
but can't they kill themselves on their own time?
I've got to get to work. I need the trains to run on time.

Politics

My embarrassment has always been conformity.
I wear deodorant like everyone else. No, there aren't
many anarchist meetings here in the suburbs.
Student loans, car loans, a mortgage—because
you can see through it, the muzzle doesn't look
like a trap. Is that the clap-riddled spectre of liberalism
I see before me, raising its skirts? Okay, but don't kiss me
on the mouth. I mean, what would Phil Ochs say?

T.h.i.s. p.o.e.m.

Some pith, some hep, some pep
to tip the hips—the smoothest tempo
pimps the emptiest thots. A heist,

it stoops to impose its otiose ethos,
its soppiest mottoes. It shops the pissiest epithets.

Poiesis epitomises its time,
emits pomposities, omits pieties.

Shit.

I mope, ashamed.

Some host, this hotshot poet.

reactionary
senates
temper
unconcerned
voters
while
xenelasic
yahoos
zeroize
alphabets
breathing
consumerism's
democracy
exorbitantly
frees
gives
humanity
individualism
jingoists
knockabout
lazar
masses
noing
one-big-unionism
poorality
quacksalvered

Deceptive, both simple and complex. A technological artefact from a world made of weight. Complicated to make, the baby sits in her dress and strokes the cat. The reading was interminable, with old white man following old white man to the podium. Gods whose words dripped heavy with the enclosing amber. The generosity of such donors a relatively recent creation. The salamander rules his world of fire, brimstone lungs lucky with clear, liquid smoke. Unknown artists delighted in meeting their mockers, my grin held tightly behind my hand. Curatorial staffs purchase important paperweights for the very large books on the subject, those that were devastatingly reliable. These Colettes, too proud of their small frozen gardens. A suburb of Paris rules the modern world, living by fire with cords of damp wood. A symbol for firefighters as well, a modern interpretation of the salamander is shown on page 109. What is a paperweight? The existential question of our times, though few are of award-winning quality. The hazard of a draft from an open window. Necessity is the other of invention, the camera lens sees all. Queen Victoria inspired a generation of popular literacy, of pornography, of desk paraphernalia to accompany ink and paper. Advice for the newly literate: the wording of a regret betrays to the well-bred the degree or absence of good-breeding. On January 10th, 1840, Parliament accepted Rowland Hill's suggestion of a prepaid uniform rate of postage by weight, thus ruining it for everyone. The open window dominated the desk before the introduction of the electric light. The Victorians, foolish fools, just wanted to look at something beautiful. A person. Who has self-respect as well as respect for others? Should never carelessly write a letter *or*. Note. Factories weighted down under demand. Solid, they feature domes decorated with elements inside. Scrambled

CANE WITH KNOB, ITALIAN, EXHIBITED EXHIBITIONS OF GOLD MEDALS AND ORDINARY COMMERCIAL TECHNOLOGY. *The Power of language must be directed towards language. The eye must see its blind spot. The prison must imprison itself.* LUXURY ITEMS SATISFIED. SMALL JEWELS BECAME FASHIONABLE. THE UPPER AND MIDDLE CLASSES RULE THE POPULAR ACTIVITY OF LETTER-WRITING AT THE HEIGHT OF ITS COMMERCE. *Only thus will the prisoners be able to make their way out.* GOOD BREEDING MAKES GOOD NEIGHBOURS. THE BACCHUS FACTORY LEADING THE WAY. THESE YEARS. KNOWN. AS THE CLASSIC. PERIOD. INDIVIDUALS INDEPENDENTLY PURSUING THEIR OWN.

xenization
yo-yoes
zugunruhe's
avifauna
bustling
canaries
decamp
eiders
flee
goldfinches
hasten

i
jadedly
kettle
letters
migrate
names
overwinter
phrases
quail
resouvenancing
sounds
towards
unsuspected
verbicidal
windows

Kremlinologists
like—
meh
no
one
providing
quips
rationally
similizing

two
unreconcilable
vocables
warrants
xenodochy
yugen
zincifies
and
bulwarks
communication
defends
expression
from
garrulous
harangues
ignominy's
jaw-holes

(EXISTENTIALISTS WANT TO KNOW, WHAT IS A PAPERWEIGHT?

C L A S S I F Y   B Y   S I Z E
A S   W E L L   A S   D E C O R
A T I O N .   E X P E R T S   A
G R E E ,   A   S P E C I A L
V O C A B U L A R Y   I S   N E
C E S S A R Y   T O   D E S C R
I B E   A N D   I D E N T I F Y
.   T H E R E   A R E   T R A D
I T I O N A L   S I Z E S .   A
P R E P A R E D   R O D   W I
T H   S P I R A L L I N G   T H
R E A D S   O N   I T S   S U R
F A C E ,   O R   A N   E N C L
O S E D   P A T T E R N   R U N
N I N G   I T S   F U L L   L E
N G T H   A N D   V I S I B L E
O N L Y   W H E N   S E E N   I
N   C R O S S - S E C T I O N ?
R E D U C E   T O   A   S U I T
A B L E   S I Z E .   B E G I N
A T   T H E   F U R N A C E .
A T   A L L   M O M E N T S ,
T H E   I M A G I N A T I O N
M U S T   K E E P   T H E   A E
S T H E T I C   C O R E   O F
T H E   C O N C E P T   T A N T
A M O U N T   A B O V E   A L L
O T H E R   C O N S I D E R A T
I O N S   O R   G R A V I T Y
W I L L   N O T   A C C E P T
T H I S   P R E C O C I O U S N
E S S   O F   A   C R E A T E D
W   E   I   G   H   T .

DIAMETER, HEIGHT, LENGTH, WIDTH, AND OTHER MEASUREMENTS AS WELL.

Politics

It's as simple as when
to use *smell, scent,* or *perfume,*
this decision to say *blood,*
obey, or *obey.*
Pull down the bottle,
pass it around; dole out the truths
you've so devotedly found.
The rhyme is how we know
our play is done, and it's time to
leave. Provide choice and the illusion
of choice. Nostalgia is a weapon
of the ruling class. Sure, but why
do we want to kill
two birds, anyway?

this poem is a conqueror of bread.
this poem still finds karl the funniest marx brother.
this poem, in its majestic equality, forbids the rich as well as the poor to sleep under bridges, to beg in the streets, and to steal bread.
this poem leveled the levelers, dug out the diggers, and ranted at the ranters.
this poem made life safe for capitalism when it drove the anarchists from the first international house of pancakes.
this poem weebled the wobblies 'til they all fell down.
this poem dreams of a land filled with women of gold, Russian nobles who walked away from their rubles, Italians who knew the revolutionary haste, and proud Frenchmen who started it all.
this poem would have scabbed for Pullman.
this is the most interesting poem in the world. after a long day of wage slavery, this poem doesn't always want an opiate—but when it does, this poem prefers the opiate of the masses.
this poem talks of voting for Debs but would have made an X for Wilson.
this poem will eventually surpass the Joneses.
this poem fears capital and for good reasons. Capital punishment and capital gains—literal death and taxes. Capital ideas.
this poem years ago recognized its kinship with all living beings, and it made up its mind that it was not a bit better than the meanest on earth. this poem said then, and says now, that while there is a lower class, this poem is in it, and while there is a criminal element this poem is of it, and while there is a soul in prison, this poem is not free.
But this poem says a lot of things.

Now
oratorship's
political
querimonious
realisms
smugly
tuck
underneath
verisimilitude
wend
xenagogues
yackety
zakating
approximating
baroque
chatter
deafening
ears'
fulsome
guerdon
how
inconceivable
jettisoning
kakistocracy's
loitering
mimesis

This is the question of this.

Is
this
this is
is this coy
this is a copy
this is a copy of this
this original copy of this
this is nowhere now here
this is neither, here nor there
this is to say is there no here in where
this is its secret but it is not the secret of this
this is not language, so that this is not this this is it

Politics

Only officials believe
the official story.
Such a quaint
slogan, I say, and so
much like Pound's
railing (*kick against*
the pricks, he said, if I
remember it rightly—
a Biblical quote,
I have always thought
but have never actually
checked though it would
be easy now to do so)
totally quaint and, I suspect,
completely appropriate.

vertiginously
wankered
x-rated
yen
zillions
aggrandized
billions
carnalized
dearly
each
frisky
greenback
humping
interestedly
joyously
kinkily
laissez-faire
munificent
nobility
often
proffers
quixotic
roleplay
sexationally
tricking
unions

T H I S

H h i I

$\neq$

A h a H

T H A T

Alas
biolinguistics
cannot
duly
explain
feverish
grunts
hummed
instances
judiciously
krakened
loquacities
manifolded
nomenclatures
only
partially
quislingly
recognized
seen
tumbling
under-abyss
veiled
wyvern
Xanadus
yelling
zeroables

P
o
l e
i   t
t   i   r
i   c   y
c   s
s

AREN'T WE ALL SUBJECTS OF THE ROMAN EMPIRE? CHANGE THE TITLE IF YOU WISH, THE SENTENCE REMAINS THE SAME. CANEWORK MADE FOR THE WEALTHY, HIGHLY DECORATIVE. BY THE 1700S THE ENGLISH TOOK UP THE CHALLENGE. SO MANY SCATTERED FLOWERS. DECANTERS, CARAFES AND TRAYS, THIN SLICES OF MILLEFIORI ENHANCED GILDED STEMS AND LEAVES. DRAWN-OUT COLOURS REDUCE THE DIAMETER WITHOUT DESTROYING THE PATTERN. EYES NEARLY ALWAYS STARE BACK. FROM THE EASTERN END OF THE MEDITERRANEAN SMALL HEADS WERE FIRED FOR USE AS JEWELLERY. LARGE GROUPS OF FIGURES TOOK THE FORM OF GODS AND GODDESSES, FASHIONED FOR THE DESSERT TABLE WHILE OTHERS RELATING TO THE BIBLE WERE USED FOR PRIVATE DEVOTIONS. EXAMPLES FROM THE 20TH CENTURY INCLUDE THOSE HUNDREDS OF THOUSANDS OF ANIMALS AND PERFUME BOTTLES, SOME MEMORIALIZED. THERE ARE MASTERS AND THERE ARE SLAVES. *time is the fire in which we burn*, AND FLUX IS THE CHEMICAL THAT LOWERS THE MELTING POINT. DEFINITIONS MADE ENTIRELY OF WHITE PORCELAIN CAMEOS, BUT THERE ARE THREE MAIN EXCEPTIONS TO THE RULE. THE EXTREMELY HIGH MOLTEN TEMPERATURES DESTROY EVERYTHING ELSE. HOW DO YOU INVENT A PROTO-PAPERWEIGHT? FIND A NEW USE FOR ROCK. IT'S IMPOSSIBLE TO KNOW IF THE RECURRANCE OF WAR IS AN ACCEPTANCE OF THE NATURALNESS OF DEATH OR THE COMPLETE REFUSAL OF THE CONCEPT OF DEATH. MELTED INTO MOUNDS, GOLD FOIL MEDALLIONS SHOW THE WORLD YOUR BRAVERY. THE FRENCH LEGION OF HONOUR WAITS AT THE BOTTOM OF YOUR TUMBLER. THE ENCAPSULATED IMMACULATE CONCEPTION SITS ON YOUR DESK, THE VIRGIN STANDING ON A CRESCENT MOON SUPPORTED BY CLOUDS AND FOUR WELL-FED CHERUBS. LEDA KISSES THE SWAN AND PULLS HIM FURTHER INSIDE WITH HER HAND. I'VE BEEN LIVING IN A NEW ELIZABETHAN AGE ALL MY LIFE AND DIDN'T EVEN KNOW IT.

this
and
this
and
and
this

probing
quietly
rummaging
skunk
twilit
Ursprache
verbarians
would
xenotransplant
you
zoologically
alter
beautifully
crepuscular
deedings
eluding
forever
grappling
hermeneutics
into
jailed
kenning
lowell's
madly
naveled
oneism

words [Politics]

i believe in
their honesty
their treacheries which
is their honesty

the word
its mysteries of trinity
and transubstantiation
spelled
differently in
different guise
every
little
logos is
you
our
human compact
the glorious conversation
we enter
small letters added
to a grand collage
a great concord
of concatenation divisible
as indivisible as
any

This
  is
this
  is
this

YOULL SEE IT WHEN YOU KNOW IT SILHOUETTES OF BIRDS AND ANIMALS CATCH THE EYE PINK SNAKES AND HALFBLIND BUTTERFLIES WAIT PATIENTLY FOR A MOMENT THAT WILL NEVER COME   A SMALL STAR CLUSTER AT THE HEART OF THE MUSHROOM THE WHITE PROFILE OF A MAN THAT COULD BE PUNCH OR THE KING OF FRANCE   WHAT DOES A MASK DO BUT MASK PAGE AFTER PAGE OF PURPLE DAHLIAS AND BLUE CLEMATIS ORANGE PANSIES AND WHITE CHAMOMILE A LAZY BEAUTY THAT REQUIRES THE INSULIN SHOCK TO THE SYSTEM   IS ART AT THE HEART OF THE REVOLUTION OR IS EVOLUTION PROVING IT ALL POINTLESS   WHAT WILL THIS PINK ROSE WEIGH DOWN AFTER THESE SCATTERED PAGES LIE LIKE DEAD PETALS IN THE SOIL   A QUESTION EVERY BIT AS ABSURD AS POETRY IN AN AGE OF MECHANICAL REPRODUCTION   WHEN I OPENED MY WINDOW LAST NIGHT I HEARD THE KANTIAN SUBLIME SIGHING EXTRAVAGANTLY WAITING TO BE NOTICED SO IT COULD TURN FLAMBOYANTLY AWAY THE ONLY STANCE ONE CAN ATTRIBUTE TO AUDEN ANTIN SAID IS THE MILD CONTRAPPOSTO OF ONE HAND IN HIS POCKET THE OTHER HOLDING A MARTINI   85 YEARS OF EARLY AMERICAN PAPERWEIGHTS PROPPED UP BY ENTICING SKILLED WORKERS FROM EUROPE TO MOVE TO NEW ENGLAND   NICOLAS MADE FLAMEWORK FRUIT AND FLOWERS IN HIS BASEMENT IN HIS HOME AT NIGHT   MACHINES DID NOT DO AWAY WITH THE PAPERWEIGHT THOUGH THEY ENDED THE CAREERS OF MANY WORKERS   THE NEW MECHANICALLY MADE BLOCK STYLES WERE IDEALLY SUITED FOR PROMOTIONAL ADVERTISING   THROUGH SUCH SPECTACLES SOME CAN SEE THE FUTURE OTHERS SEE ONE BIG UNION I SEE THE PAGE AND ALL OF ITS BULLSHIT AND IN ENTERTAINMENT NEWS HALLOWEEN CAME EARLY THIS YEAR TO MOSTLY BAD REVIEWS

Politics

Words-ward
raw war
draws arrows
swords
playing
language's game
and striking out

prime numbers
minister out
calculated silence
words sliding
comically underfoot just
ice

So sorrow awards dross

Was a sad ado—
or
do-do-do do-waa?

this
utterance
vociferant
waves'
xenoglossic
yelps
zeroing
at
beatific
creations
drowns
embryonic
futures
gauleiter
haphazardly
incontestably
jaundicing
knowingness
language
menaces
noyading
opportune
possibilities
quietation
resignedly
sentenced

CANADA HAD NO TRADITION OF ELABORATE PAPERWEIGHTS IN THE 19TH CENTURY CANADA ITS POPULATION TOO SMALL TO SUPPORT LARGE FACTORIES WITH LARGE SKILLED WORK FORCES CANADA EVEN IN THE 1870S RELYING ON GOVERNMENT SANCTIONS AND TARIFFS TO CREATE HOMEGROWN BUSINESS CANADIANS ENTHUSIASTICALLY ACCEPTED THE REINVENTED PAPERWEIGHT FORMS OFTEN USED FOR PROMOTIONAL ADVERTISING OR FOR LOCAL ATTRACTIONS AS WITH TODAY MANY PAPERWEIGHTS RELATING TO CANADA WERE MADE IN OTHER COUNTRIES WHAT DOES OLD CITY HALL THINK OF THAT

Politics [Words]

Civilization is tumbling
as it always has been and will be,
and the words are always right there, pushing

and pulling.

You would have heard
Reagan's nine most terrifying words,
Carlin's seven words you can't say on tv,
these words and so many more, all,
all you invited into the grand collage.

But I am a man of my betrayals,
there is no Eleusinian mystery
to that much, at least.
In the beginning the word was
even then, on the slant deathward,
building its scaffold of words.
Often I am permitted to return
to a meadow... a made place, created...
of words within words...

All of this, the site of my casual betrothals.
Only words come into it, Robert.
These words are our sentence.

THERESACERTAINBRILLIANTLACKOFCONCERNBUILINGAPAPERWEI
GHTDOORSTOPMUCHLIKETHEWOODENFIREESCAPESPLENTIFULINTHE
MARITIMESLOWDOMESANDCOLOUREDTRANSPARENCIESREFLECTTHE
NEWAGEOFBELIEFCHRISTONACRACKERAPEARONACOOKIEBACCHUS
ANDSONSPREFERREDTHEMAGNUMSIZESBLESSEDARETHECHEESEMAK
ERSAFTERALLWORDSTOLIVEBYJUSTBECAUSEYOUCANTSEEITDOESNT
MEANYOUWONTHAVETOCLEANUPTHEDEADBIRDSBENEATHITONEFIS
HTWOFISHREDFISHBOILINGSEAASKILLEDCRAFTSMANHADHISHANDIN
THATTHEINKWELLDISPLAYSANELEMENTOFFUNHOWBESTTOSOLVETH
EPROBLEMOFTHREEWHITEMICEBUTONLYTWOPIECESOFCHEDDARSIX
HOTPOKERSTOTHEEYESITSHARDTOFEELSADTHEWORLDSCORALISDYI
NGWHENIJUSTFOUNDOUTITWASALIVEGIVENTHECHOICEWHOWOULD
NTWANTTOBETRAPPEDINAMBER

Politics

, a Vision of a Dream. A Fragmentation.

I sit here writing an ode for the age
called *Love in the Time of Late Capitalism.*

In Flanders fields did One Percent
A stately pleasure dome decree:
Where Blood, the sacred river, ran
Through caverns measureless to man
   Down to a sunless sea.

Enough.

This is a thing of ugly.

I conjugate our species as
my
mine
mined
moan.

The whole point of Batman is to take our attention away
from all the Bruce Waynes of the world.

It is not rocket science.
This writing thing is as simple as when to use *smell,*
scent, or *perfume,* the decision to say *obey, obey,*
or *obey.*

Two roads terminated
in a yellow wood.

Yes, all we need is love,
but sometimes our love is hate.

The world is doomed, just as it
has always been; the only choice we have
is whether to believe that.

I love this first-person singular, so quaint.
Then it's over—the rhyme is how we know
the play is done, and it is time to go.

Politics

Yes, all this champagne socialism can be exhausting,
running around like a simile with its head cut off,
the hamster wagging the dog, the tail running its wheel.
Politics as circle jerk? Yes,
I, too, dislike it.

On the way to my office, there is a long, windowed corridor running along the front of several buildings. Over the course of one winter, it seemed I watched a sparrow starve to death in that glassed warmth. Is it fair to say the sparrow of desire has flitted to the fields of a more delicate menagerie? No. It is the slip that reveals too much. I have always thought *stained* was an odd way to describe such beauty, especially a beauty our forerunners dedicated to their God.

This simple

And now let us turn, at last, to simple speech.
Simply, we turn to speech, and it lets us.
To speak, simply turn and let us at last begin.
Let us begin to speak, turning simply now over and over.
Speech, over and over, simply turning us away now.
Now, simply, over and over, turns us away. To speak of this. At last.

"When the point is to try to present that there is something that is not presentable, you have to make presentation suffer" (Jean-François Lyotard, *The Inhuman*, 125).

this
is the
immanence
in the
imminence

Acknowledgements

Poems from this work have previously appeared in the periodicals *BafterC* and *New American Writing;* "This is a small poem for Robert Kroetsch" was included in the chapbook *Dear Robert Kroetsch*; the poems in "Concatenations" were published in a chapbook of the same name by above/ground press; the poems in "ssalGlass" appeared in the online magazine *17 seconds*. My thanks to the editors.

Stephen Cain, Steve McOrmond, and Matthew Tierney all provided much-needed support and encouragement throughout the writing of this book. Adam Dickinson supplied a number of necessary comments, distractions, laughs, and insights. Christine McNair and rob mclennan believed in this book when few others did; I am extremely grateful.

This is for Kelly Laycock and equally for Duncan Weaver, the new this that Kelly created during the creation of *this*. These two are my this.

Andy Weaver is the author of two previous books of poetry: *were the bees* (NeWest, 2005) and *gangson* (NeWest, 2011). He teaches contemporary poetry and poetics at York University. His home life is dominated by the rule of ones: one wife, one son, one cat, one dog, and one house plant. All are lovely.

Library and Archives Canada Cataloguing in Publication

Weaver, Andy, 1971-, author
This / Andy Weaver.

Poems.
ISBN 978-1-928107-06-4 (paperback)

I. Title.

PS8595.E175T45 2015 C811'.6 C2015-906145-8

WWW.CHAUDIEREBOOKS.COM

Colophon

This book was typeset in Minion and Courier by Christine McNair using Adobe InDesign. Minion is a serif typeface designed by Robert Slimbach and inspired by late Renaissance-era type. The name comes from the traditional naming system for type sizes, in which minion is between nonpareil and brevier, equivalent to modern 7PT type. Slimbach described the design as having "a simplified structure and moderate proportions." Courier is a monospaced slab serif typeface designed to resemble the output from a strike-on typewriter. The typeface was designed by Howard "Bud" Kettler in 1955, and it was later redrawn by Adrian Frutiger for the IBM Selectric Composer series of electric typewriters.